Try This AT Home!

Impressive Dance Moves

Ellen Labrecque

Raintree

Chicago, Illinois

Edited by Rebecca Rissman, Daniel Nunn, and Adrian Vigliano
Designed by Cynthia Della-Rovere
Picture research by Elizabeth Alexander
Production by Alison Parsons
Originated by Capstone Global Library Ltd.
Printed and bound in China by China Translation and Printing Services Ltd.

16 15 14 13 12
10 9 8 7 6 5 4 3 2 1

Library of Congress Cataloging-in-Publication Data

Labrecque, Ellen.

  Impressive dance moves / Ellen Labrecque.

     p. cm.—(Try this at home!)

  Includes bibliographical references and index.

  ISBN 978-1-4109-5004-8 (hb)—ISBN 978-1-4109-5011-6 (pb) 1. Dance—Juvenile literature. I. Title.

  GV1596.5.L34 2013

  792.8—dc23   2012014404

Acknowledgments

The author and publisher are grateful to the following for permission to reproduce copyright material: © Capstone Publishers pp. 8 t, 8 b, 9 t, 9 b, 10, 11, 12, 13 t, 13 b, 14 t, 14 b, 15 t, 15 b, 16 t, 16 b, 17, 18, 19 t, 19 b, 20, 21 t, 21 b, 22, 23 t, 23 b, 24 t, 24 b, 25 t, 25 b, 26, 27 t, 27 b (Karon Dubke); Getty images pp. 4 (Granger Wootz/Blend Images), 28 (Image Source), 29 (altrendo images/Stockbyte); SuperStock pp. 5 (© fStop), 6 (© Richard B. Levine/Ambient Images Inc.), 7 (© Image Source). Design features reproduced with the permission of Shutterstock (© CAN BALCIOGLU), (© Nadezda), (© Merve Poray), (© Nicemonkey).

Cover photograph of a modern style dancer reproduced with permission of Shutterstock (© Ayakovlev).

Every effort has been made to contact copyright holders of any material reproduced in this book. Any omissions will be rectified in subsequent printings if notice is given to the publisher.

All the Internet addresses (URLs) given in this book were valid at the time of going to press. However, due to the dynamic nature of the Internet, some addresses may have changed, or sites may have changed or ceased to exist since publication. While the author and publisher regret any inconvenience this may cause readers, no responsibility for any such changes can be accepted by either the author or the publisher.

Bloomington, Chicago, Mankato, Oxford

Contents

Some words are shown in bold, **like this**. You can find out what they mean by looking in the Glossary.

Let's Dance!

Everybody and anybody can dance. The trick is to look good while doing it. How do you do that? By learning the coolest moves around!

Your friends will want to groove just like you after you master the moves in this book. All you need to do is practice. Let's get ready to boogie, rock, shimmy, and dance the night and day away!

Be Safe

You don't need a helmet or safety pads for dancing. But you should wear comfortable clothing and shoes, so that you can move around easily without tripping or falling.

Dancing is exercise—you may even work up a sweat. If you want to dance, it is important to stay fit. And don't forget to take rest breaks and drink plenty of water to stay **hydrated**. Then, you can get back on the dance floor and get going. Let's learn some moves!

The Spin

STEP 1

The spin is simple. First, bend your knees slightly and put your hands out to your side to help you stay balanced.

STEP 2

To spin to your left, plant your left foot behind your right and turn your upper body to the right to gain **momentum**.

8

Lift your right foot and bring it around your body as you keep your left toes planted.

Spin to the **beat** of the song.

Spin your body all the way around to face the same direction. Step out with your right foot to stop spinning.

Moonwalk

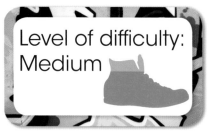

Level of difficulty:
Medium

The moonwalk was made popular by **legendary** pop star Michael Jackson.

STEP **1**

To begin, lift your left leg so that only your toes are on the floor.

STEP 2

Place your right foot about 12 inches (30 cm) in front of your left. Slide your right heel back so it is even with your left.

Snap the left heel down and raise the right heel at the same time, so that now the right toes are facing toward the floor.

Repeat this move again and again. The smoother you glide, the cooler it looks!

The Robot

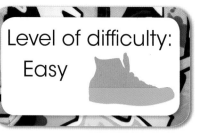

STEP 1

When you do the robot, you want to look **rigid**. Bend your arms at the elbow in a 90-degree angle. Slowly raise them, one at a time, so that your open palms reach eye level.

Slowly turn your head from right to left, again and again.

STEP 2

Now try walking. As you raise one arm, take a step, keeping your legs bent slightly at the knees.

STEP 3

While keeping your back **taut**, stiffly bend at the waist once in a while to add flair to the dance.

Crisscross

STEP 1

Stand with your legs shoulder-width apart and your knees bent.

STEP 2

Jump straight up in the air and, as you hop up, crisscross your legs.

14

STEP 3

Jump up again and crisscross your legs the other way.

STEP 4

Land with your legs shoulder-width apart, and then rock side to side four times.

Repeat the first two steps again and face a new direction each time. This dance looks great with a big group!

The Worm

STEP 1

Lie face down on the floor and put your arms on the ground in a push-up position. Your stomach should still be on the floor.

STEP 2 Kick your legs up. Right before your legs reach the ground again, do a push-up.

16

STEP **3**

When your toes touch the ground again, kick out and do another push-up. Inch up a little bit on every move.

Make your body as loose as possible and keep repeating these steps. You want a wave-like motion to course through your body.

The Arm Wave

STEP 1

With this move, you want your body to look **fluid**. Hold both arms straight out to your side.

Begin with your right hand. Curl your hand down and raise your elbow at the same time. Lift your shoulder and straighten out your arm on an angle.

Continue the movement to the other (left) shoulder. Lift your left shoulder, then put it down and lift up your elbow.

STEP 3

Straighten out your arm and point your wrist downward. Bring the move back to the other side.

The Clown

Level of difficulty:
Medium

STEP 1

The clown uses the arm wave as part of the move. Begin by shaking both hands from the wrist like you are trying to shake water off of them.

STEP 2

As you shake your hands, bend your knees and pop up and down.

STEP 3

Go up and down four times, then switch to the arm wave.

Do the arm wave twice, then go back to the first movement. Make sure your body is loose and flowing from move to move.

21

The Tut

Level of difficulty:
Medium

STEP 1

The Tut is all about stiff-arm poses. It is most important to keep your hands flat and fingers together. Hold one arm in front of you and bend it at the elbow at a right angle. Then bend your flat palm down at another right angle.

STEP 2

Bend your other arm the opposite way. Your forearm is pointing down, and your flat palm is pointing behind you.

STEP 3

Take small, stiff steps forward.

Everyday Moves

STEP 1

You can **imitate** real-life stuff and do it on the dance floor! Spin around like a sprinkler.

STEP 2

Pretend to shop at a grocery store. Push the cart along and reach up high for "food" on the shelves. Put it into your cart.

24

Pretend to sprinkle your food with salt and pepper. Hold a shaker in each hand.

STEP 4

Pretend to bake a cake. Stir all the ingredients together. Put your whole body into the stirring motion.

Melting

Melting is a way to move from one dance move to another. Move slowly when you melt. To practice, start by standing straight with your arms up in the air.

Next, start to lean back and bend your knees to bring your whole body down slowly.

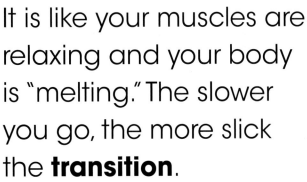

STEP 3

It is like your muscles are relaxing and your body is "melting." The slower you go, the more slick the **transition**.

How to Look Smooth

You want to look **fluid** on the dance floor. Here are five tips for how to look your best.

1. Listen to the music. The more aware you are of the **tempo** and **beat**, the better you'll do.

2. The best dancers are the ones who dance like nobody is watching.